Katie's feet seemed to be dancing as they dangled from her seat on the big yellow school bus, swaying back and forth as she waited for her sister's arrival. It had been a happy day all day long; even the sun seemed to be smiling.

"Hi, Kristen!" Katie called to her sister as she hurried down the aisle.

It would only be a brief ride before the bus would stop at the corner of Steven Place, and Katie and Kristen would scamper out of the bus with the other children for the short walk home.

Katie couldn't wait to tell Kristen about her school picture. Her mommy had allowed her to wear her favorite navy blue dress with red stripes on the shoulders and bright gold stars on the big white collar. Katie loved that dress, but she loved her shiny white patent leather party shoes even more. She liked the way they felt on her feet. They made her toes giggle and want to dance. She would tap her feet on the kitchen floor and twirl around like a ballerina. She liked the rapping sound they made when the soles of her shoes hit the tiled floor. Those shoes were special.

Katie started to talk as soon as her sister slid into the seat beside her.

"Well," said Katie. "Don't you want to know about my picture?"

Katie's curly brown pigtails that were tied in red, white, and blue bows to match her dress, swung back and forth as Katie bounced in her seat.

"Okay, okay!" Kristen said.

Katie proceeded to tell Kristen about the photographer whose favorite phrase seemed to be, 'Say cheese!' and his assistant, who gave the students a choice of three things they could hold in their hands for the photo. There was a book, a toy, or paintbrushes.

Katie proudly blurted out, "I picked the paintbrushes! That's why I'm calling it 'My Painting Picture.'"

Kristen rolled her eyes. "Katie, you're the only kid I know who actually *names* their school picture."

The bus slowly came to a stop. The door made a *phisshhh* sound when the bus driver, Mrs. Phillips, opened it. "See you tomorrow!" She waved to the kids as they exited the bus. Katie jumped off the bus first. Suddenly, she didn't like the way her feet felt. They felt like they were stuck in something squishy. Her toes weren't giggling this time. There, on the grass at the bus stop was a big pile of dog poop, and Katie was standing right in the middle of it! She tried to wipe it off on the grass, but the more she tried, the more dog poop clung to her shoes.

Georgie P. pushed her out of the way. "Hey, everyone, look!" he shouted. "Katie stepped in dog poop, and boy does it stink!!" All the kids laughed and held their noses.

Kristen grabbed Katie's hand, "Come on, Katie. Ignore Georgie P. He's just a dumb boy." Katie and Kristen walked home as fast as they could.

When they got to their house, they sat down on the steps. Kristen put her arm around Katie's shoulder. "Katie, don't be sad."

Katie pushed her sister's arm off her shoulder. "NO! I will never wear these stinky poop shoes again! I hate them!"

She unbuckled her shoes and tossed them aside.

"Come on, Katie," Kristen said. "Daddy will be home soon. He'll clean up your shoes."

Katie shook her head back and forth. "I don't care," she said to her sister, "I will never wear those stinky, smelly, dirty, ugly, poop shoes again. YUCK! I hate them!"

Kristen shrugged. "Okay, Katie, they're your shoes. I'm going in the house."

Katie sat on the step without any shoes. Her toes were not dancing anymore. She stood up while she held her nose with two fingers from her left hand. With her right hand, she leaned down and *very* carefully picked up the two smelly shoes. She held them as far away from her as she could walking quickly, but cautiously, toward the trashcan at the curb on the street corner. She leaned the shoes up against the can, turned around, and went back to the steps and sat down. *There, she thought, no more poop shoes for me!*

The way those shoes looked propped up against the trashcan made her sad. They looked lonely. Katie remembered how she used to love to tap, tap, tap, with her shoes on the kitchen floor. But that was before they became poop shoes.

She heard the front door open behind her and glanced up to see her mother. "Katie, why are you being so silly? Your father will clean those shoes, and they'll be as good as new."

Katie didn't move. She stared at the trashcan and said, "Nope, I'm NOT wearing them."

"Well then, young lady," her mother said firmly. "If you throw those shoes away, I won't be buying you new ones anytime soon. The choice is yours, Katie." She went back into the house.

"I don't care," Katie said.

Georgie P. held his nose as he rode past her house on his bike. Katie rested her chin on her hand and sighed. Now she hated the poop shoes even more.

Hi Katie!" Daddy called as he got out of his plumbing truck. He sat down next to her on the steps while she told him her sad story.

"You know, Katie," he said. "I think I can fix this for you…"

"N-O, NO!" Katie cried out. Her raised voice caused Miss Carolyn, who lived next door, to peek around the fence to see what all the commotion was about.

Miss Carolyn was puttering around her garden like she often did on nice days. Anyone who knew Miss Carolyn knew two things about her; she loved to garden and she loved to bake.

Daddy waved to Miss Carolyn as he stood up to go into the house. "Well, Katie," he said. "It sounds like *you've* made your decision." He patted Katie on the head as he turned to go inside. Katie could hear her dog, Murphy barking hello to her Daddy as he scratched behind the dog's ears like he always did. Katie felt sad as she sat alone on the step.

Georgie P. rode by again, holding his nose. Katie really hoped that he'd fall off his bike.

The house was quiet that night while everyone slept, everyone but Katie. She tossed and turned in her bed until she finally threw off her blanket and wiggled her toes. Her sudden movement stirred Murphy, who was curled up beside her bed. He opened his eyes and lifted his head when Katie swung her legs over the side of the bed.

"Shhhh!" Katie held her finger to her lips as she slipped out of her bed and crouched down next to Murphy.

"Shhhh," she said quietly as she stroked the top of his head. Murphy yawned and went back to sleep.

Katie tiptoed to the bedroom window. Pushing the curtain aside, she looked out into the night. *It's funny,* she thought, *how sunshine can make you feel warm and happy, and then the moon comes out, and you feel cold and lonely.* Katie looked over toward the corner where the trashcans stood near the streetlight. A gentle breeze picked up a small piece of paper and blew it across the grass where it got stuck inside one of the shoes. Her shoes…the poop shoes.

Katie let the curtain fall back into place, and she sat on the edge of her bed. A big sigh pushed itself out of her chest and into the air, where it seemed to stay for a long time. Even if her father cleaned up her shoes, it wouldn't matter. They weren't the same.

"Nope." Katie sighed softly as she lay back in her bed. "It just wouldn't be the same." Murphy opened one eye and wagged his tail. He turned his head and went back to sleep.

The next school day came and went, and as Katie followed her sister off the bus, she noticed the poop shoes still propped up against the trashcan. She tried to avoid looking at them, but as much as she tried, she just had to look. A few more pieces of paper had found their way inside the shoes, and a big fat bug was crawling across the left shoe strap, which only made her feet feel sadder.

"Hi Katie!" A familiar voice called out her name, which made her look around.

"How are you today?"

Katie looked in the direction of Miss Carolyn's house but couldn't see anyone.

"Over here, Katie!" Suddenly, just above the top of the fence, a sunhat appeared along with some fingertips.

"It's me, Miss Carolyn!"

Miss Carolyn laughed. Katie smiled and walked toward the fence dragging her backpack along with her. As long as her family had lived on Steven Place, Miss Carolyn had been their neighbor. She was always there to lend a helping hand, and she had the prettiest house and garden on the street. When the weather was nice, she would almost always be outside working in her flower beds or her fruit and vegetable garden. When the weather was cold, she'd use the things that she'd grown all summer to bake tasty pies and cookies. *Yummy,* thought Katie, *That's how Miss Carolyn's house smelled on a cold and snowy day.*

Seeing Miss Carolyn standing there in her garden with her sunhat on took Katie's mind off her poop shoes. She almost felt happy.

"Well, hello there, Katie!" Miss Carolyn was saying as she put on her floral gardening gloves.

"Hi, Miss Carolyn!" Katie said.

Miss Carolyn stood by a pile of leaves and scraps she had just arranged into a mound under a tree in her yard. It looked like a small multi-colored mountain. There were green leaves, brown leaves, pieces of old fruit, apple peels, orange peels, peach pits, and other fruit skins.

Katie didn't want to seem impolite, especially to a grown-up, but she thought it was strange that Miss Carolyn was saving discarded food and rubbish.

"Miss Carolyn?"

Miss Carolyn threw some other old scraps onto the top of the heap.

"Yes, Katie? Is there something on your mind?"

Katie paused for a few seconds before asking, "Well, I was just wondering why you're saving this pile of junk?"

"Junk!" Miss Carolyn giggled. "This isn't junk Katie. This is a compost heap."

"A what?"

"A compost heap."

Katie shook her head. "What are you going to use that for?"

Miss Carolyn began sorting through some scraps on the table where she kept her gardening tools and materials. "Katie," she said. "Go ask your mother if you can come over and visit for a while."

Katie grabbed her backpack and ran to ask her mother if it would be okay. She hurried right back to Miss Carolyn's after promising her mother she'd behave.

"Wow, Katie," Miss Carolyn said. "You're fast!" She picked up some apple peels and peach skins. "You see these? You think that this is junk. The apples and peaches have already been eaten, so why not just throw these out, right?"

"Right!" Katie said with a smile.

"Wrong!" Miss Carolyn said. "There are still nutrients in these skins that are good for the soil."

Katie's mouth opened in surprise. "*Really*, Miss Carolyn?"

"Oh, yes, indeed!" Miss Carolyn pointed to the pile. "After a while, I'll take the compost and spread it around the flowers and trees in my gardens. It's called mulching." She handed Katie some old fruit skins. "You want to try it?"

Katie jumped at the chance to help, "Sure!" It was fun tossing scraps of fruit and leaves on the little compost mountain.

Miss Carolyn opened up the small shed she kept in her yard. Katie stayed outside the shed's open doors. "WOW!" she said as she looked inside. There were shelves of jars with all kinds of things in them.

There were nails, screws, tacks, and bottle caps. There was a bag with a drawstring that had tipped over, and all different colors of buttons had spilled out onto one of the counter tops. The sun peeked through one of the windows of the shed. Its rays hit the scattered buttons, creating a rainbow on one of the walls.

"Look, Miss Carolyn!" Katie said.

Miss Carolyn turned around and smiled when she saw the rainbow too.

"Isn't nature wonderful, Katie? Just minutes ago, we were working in my garden, and now suddenly, a rainbow appears on the wall of my shed!"

Katie nodded.

There were other things on the shelves, too; neatly lined spools of string, old tools, small flower pots, tiny plants, and bags filled with seeds. Some of the bags were slightly torn. Some tiny seeds had fallen onto the dirt floor of the shed causing small green sprigs to sprout up.

"Miss Carolyn, where did you get all this stuff?"

Miss Carolyn pulled a fairly large bag out of the shed while she answered Katie's question. "Well," she stopped to catch her breath. "I never throw anything useful away. I recycle them. What we may think of as trash or junk may seem like a pirate's treasure to someone else."

Katie tilted her head to the side. "Really?"

Miss Carolyn pointed to the buttons. "Well, if you have all your buttons on your coat, you wouldn't think about buttons. But, if it's cold outside and you have no buttons on your coat, buttons would be very important to you."

Katie thought for a minute before answering. "I guess you're right, Miss Carolyn."

Miss Carolyn started to pull the bag again. "And those fruit scraps, skins, and leaves that people throw out? They help to make the soil rich so that I can grow my beautiful flowers."

Katie thought that Miss Carolyn was probably the smartest lady in the whole wide world and was just about to tell her when she got a whiff of something really stinky. She immediately looked down at her shoes. *Nope*, no poop on the soles of her shoes, but it sure smelled like it. "Phew!" Katie said. "What's that smell?"

Miss Carolyn dropped the bag and laughed. "It's just manure, Katie."

Katie checked her shoes again. "What's manure?"

Miss Carolyn wiped a drop of sweat from her forehead with a small handkerchief she kept in her pocket. "It's animal waste, Katie, that's all."

Now Katie was sure Miss Carolyn was the smartest lady in the world because she never heard of anything called manure or anything called animal waste, *not ever!*

Miss Carolyn laughed again. "Katie," she said. "It's poop!"

"*WHAT?*" Katie couldn't believe what she was hearing. "Poop? Manure is poop? *And* they *sell it* in a store?"

Miss Carolyn nodded. "Indeed, they *do!*" She was still smiling as she started dragging the bag of manure toward some Montauk Daisies she had planted along the fence. "These are starting to get buds on them, and they'll be in full bloom soon," she said as she pulled the string at the top of the bag to make a small opening. She began taking tiny handfuls of manure out of the bag and mixing it into the soil around the daisies. Miss Carolyn's gardening gloves didn't seem to mind having manure all over them as she pushed and poked around the daisies.

"Well, Katie," Miss Carolyn asked. "Are you going to help me or not?"

Katie hesitated. "Ah, well, ah, okay, maybe."

Miss Carolyn looked above the glasses on her nose and gave Katie a wink. "There's another pair of gardening gloves in the shed if you'd like to wear them."

Katie hurried to the open shed and found the gloves on one of the shelves. They were a little bit big, but Katie didn't mind. They made her feel like a real gardener. She was just about to kneel beside Miss Carolyn when she had an idea.

"I'll be back in a second!" Katie said as she ran off.

She was back in a flash. "I want to recycle these! Katie held up her white patent leather party shoes. "They're manure shoes, Miss Carolyn!"

And Katie told Miss Carolyn the whole story from beginning to end. When she was finished, Miss Carolyn said, "Are you sure you want to do this, Katie?"

Katie didn't hesitate. "Yep, that's what I want to do."

Miss Carolyn clapped her hands. "Well, okay then, let's get started!"

The following morning, Katie hurried to the bus stop at the corner of Steven Place with her sister. It was a happy day. The sky was blue, and the sun was smiling. Other kids were already waiting for the bus. Katie turned momentarily to look in the direction of Miss Carolyn's house. There, by the fence, nestled among the budding Montauk Daisies, was a pair of white patent leather party shoes. They already had daisies growing next to them and all around them. Inside the shoes, two very nice gardeners had replanted some daisies in rich soil, and yes, manure. It wouldn't be long before they were all in full bloom.

Katie turned back just as Mrs. Phillips was coming around the corner, driving the big yellow school bus. After a few minutes, most of the kids were seated when Katie heard Georgie P. shouting, "Wait for me!" He ran as fast as he could toward the school bus.

The bus driver held the door open for him so he could hop on, and Georgie P. sat down in the seat across from Katie and her sister for the ride to school. Within seconds, most of the kids sitting nearby began to hold their noses, asking, "Who stinks?"

The boy in the seat behind Georgie P. stood up and started to laugh as he pointed to Georgie P.'s shoes. Then someone on the bus sang out, "Georgie P. smells like dog poop," causing most of the kids on the bus to giggle and snicker. But not Katie. She didn't join in on any of the singing or teasing, and when she glanced over at Georgie P., she could see that he didn't seem to think it was one bit funny.

Mrs. Phillips stopped the bus, opened several windows, and calmly told the children to "please, sit down and be polite." She handed Georgie.P. a few paper towels to rest his feet on and advised him to go to the nurse's office and clean off his shoes as soon as he got to school.

As the bus slowly made its way past Miss Carolyn's house, Katie saw that she was already outside working in her flower and vegetable gardens. Miss Carolyn smiled and waved as the yellow bus chugged along on its way to school. Katie smiled and waved back. She could see her party shoes among the beautiful flowers. The daisies seemed to be dancing in the morning breeze, and Katie was sure she could hear them giggle and see them smile.

Glossary

Recycling: Using things that you might have thrown out to make something new or better.

Mulching: Decaying leaves, plants and fruit skins that you put in the soil to improve its quality.

Compost Heap: A pile of decaying fruit skins, plants, and leaves that is set aside for mulching.

Manure: Animal poop that's put into the soil to make it better for plants and crops to grow.

Nature: Everything around us! Things like trees, animals, earth, rocks, plants, flowers, bugs... nothing that is man-made.

Soil: The top layer of earth where plants grow.

DEDICATION

For my father George W. Plunkett Jr. "The Leader of the Band." A gifted artist and musician, we shared a love of drawing, painting, and art in all forms. And for my brother Michael Patrick, also a gifted writer and artist. Both taught me, by example, how to live life on life's terms – without regret or complaint.

ACKNOWLEDGMENTS

My mother, "Mrs. Phillips" and my brother "Georgie P." (who is *never* like the rascal in this story!) My sister, Jeannine, who tirelessly cares for all of us and without whom I would be lost. My brother-in-law Glen, the world's greatest master plumber! My nieces, Katie Rose and Kristen, my biggest cheerleaders. The faculty at The High School of Art and Design in Manhattan. Professor Lillian Thurau at Suffolk County Community College who told me long ago, "Melanie, you are a writer!" Teresa Velardi, my publisher who walked me through the publication process. Finally, to all my fellow writers in Shoreham and Patchogue N.Y. who inspire me and amaze me always. Thanks to all!

ABOUT MELANIE

From an early age, Melanie Francis loved to draw. Eventually, she earned admittance to New York City's prestigious *High School of Art and Design.*
While in college, Melanie discovered that she enjoyed writing stories as much as she liked drawing and painting. She has combined her love of art with her love of writing to create "Poop Shoes." Ms. Francis is currently working on her next children's book, "Miss Abby Crabby."

COMING SOON

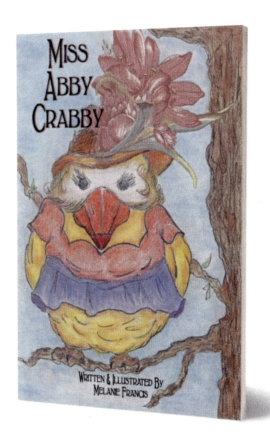

Miss Abby Crabby thought she was the big boss of everything. She wore a big hat and had an even bigger mouth! She was loud, bossy, and said mean hurtful things. But when she was cruel to Miss Sally Sparrow, the birds living in the trees surrounding the lake decided she had gone too far. The time had come to stand together against this bully!

Praise for *Poop Shoes*

"Perfect book to read with the class on Earth Day. Beautiful illustrations too! Coloring pages are an extra bonus at the end."

Bernadette Seibert, Educator

As a mom and educator, I can easily say that this book is a work of literary genius! I've long been searching for the "perfect book" to read to my three kids, and I've finally found it! "poop Shoes" is interesting and funny with a twist of meaningful lessons for children. The charming illustrations truly connect the reader to the story. Makes our hearts smile.
Highly recommend!

K. Ruthkowski, Educator

© 2020 Melanie Francis

Published in the United States of America

All rights reserved worldwide.

Authentic Endeavors Publishing / Book Endeavors

Clarks Summit PA 18411

© 2020 Illustrated by Melanie Francis

No part of this book may be reproduced by any mechanical, photographic or electronic process, or in the form of an audio or digital recording, nor may it be stored in any retrieval system, transmitted or otherwise, be copied for public or private use – other than for fair use as brief quotation embodied in articles and review - without prior written permission of the author, illustrators or publisher.

This publication is a work of fiction. Names, characters, businesses, places, events, and incidents are either the products of the author's imagination or used in a fictitious manner. Any resemblance to actual persons, living or dead or actual events or places is purely coincidental.

ISBN: 978-0-9982105-7-5

Library of Congress Control Number: 2020916629

Made in the USA
Middletown, DE
13 December 2020